WHY RICHARD KING MATTERS TO TEXAS

By Charles Cameron

Published in 2014 by The Rosen Publishing Group, Inc.
29 East 21st Street, New York, NY 10010

First Edition

Developed, written, and produced by Digital Discovery Publishing
Editors: Molly Aloian, Wendy Scavuzzo
Design & Production: Katherine Berti
Photo research: Crystal Sikkens, Allison Napier
Proofreader: Sarah Cairns

Photo Credits: Cattle Raisers Museum, Fort Worth: page 28
DeGolyer Library, Southern Methodist University, Dallas, Texas, Lawrence T. Jones III Photography Collection: page 26
The Granger Collection, NYC: cover, pages 1, 4, 3 (bottom), 19 (top)
Library of Congress: pages 12, 18, 19 (bottom), 24, 30
The Image Works: page 9 (bottom)
North Wind Picture Archives: pages 13 (top), 16, 17, 20 (top), 22
Rugeley-Moore Collection, Richmond, Texas: pages 10, 11
Shutterstock: pages 3 (middle), 25
University of Texas at San Antonio Libraries Special Collections: page 15
Wikimedia Commons: pages 7, 9 (top), 23, 27, 29

Maps by Digital Discovery Publishing: pages 5, 6

All websites were live and accurate at the time of printing.

Library of Congress Cataloging-in-Publication Data

Cameron, Charles.
Why Richard King matters to Texas / by Charles Cameron.
p. cm. -- (Texas perspectives)
Includes index.
ISBN 978-1-4777-0910-8 (library binding) -- ISBN 978-1-4777-0926-9 (pbk.) -- ISBN 978-1-4777-0927-6 (6-pack)
1. King, Richard, 1824-1885 — Juvenile literature. 2. Ranchers — Texas — Biography — Juvenile literature. 3. Ranch life — Texas — History — 19th century — Juvenile literature. 4. Cattle trade — Texas – History — 19th century — Juvenile literature. I. Title.
F391.K535 C34 2013
976.4--dc23

Manufactured in the United States of America

CPSIA Compliance Information: Batch W13PK: For Further Information contact Rosen Publishing, New York, New York at 1-800-237-9932

CONTENTS

1 CAPTAIN KING

In the spring of 1852, Richard King decided to see Corpus Christi, in Texas. Richard had been captaining steamboats up and down the Rio Grande for five years, but he had never really seen the countryside or towns north of Brownsville. He traveled for hundreds of miles (km) over sand flats through a part of southern Texas known then as the Wild Horse Desert. It was an endless, wild landscape about which little was known.

Richard King was known as Captain King for most of his life. Even his wife would call him "Captain."

After visiting the Wild Horse Desert in the early 1820s, Stephen F. Austin offered this opinion on the land:

"*...the poorest I ever saw in my life. It is generally nothing but sand, entirely void of lumber, covered with scrubby thorn bushes and prickly pear.*"

Richard soon came across endless grass plains and the waters of Santa Gertrudis Creek. Where others saw an empty, **hostile** desert Richard saw an opportunity. He carved out a thriving cattle business in this untamed wilderness. Through determination, creativity, and constant investment, King Ranch grew into an **empire** within Richard's lifetime. It remains one of the largest cattle ranches in the world today and maintains a mythic place in Texas history.

Texas Perspective

Richard King grew his ranching empire to more than 600,000 acres (242,811 ha) in his lifetime. His efforts launched the cattle ranching industry in Texas.

RICHARD KING'S TEXAS

2 EARLY YEARS

Richard King was born on July 10, 1824, in New York. Not much is known about his early life, except that his parents came to North America from Ireland and were very poor. When Richard was five years old his parents died, and he was sent to live with an aunt. He became a jeweler's **apprentice** at age nine but he did not like working for the jeweler and ran away. Richard found a ship headed south and hid away on it.

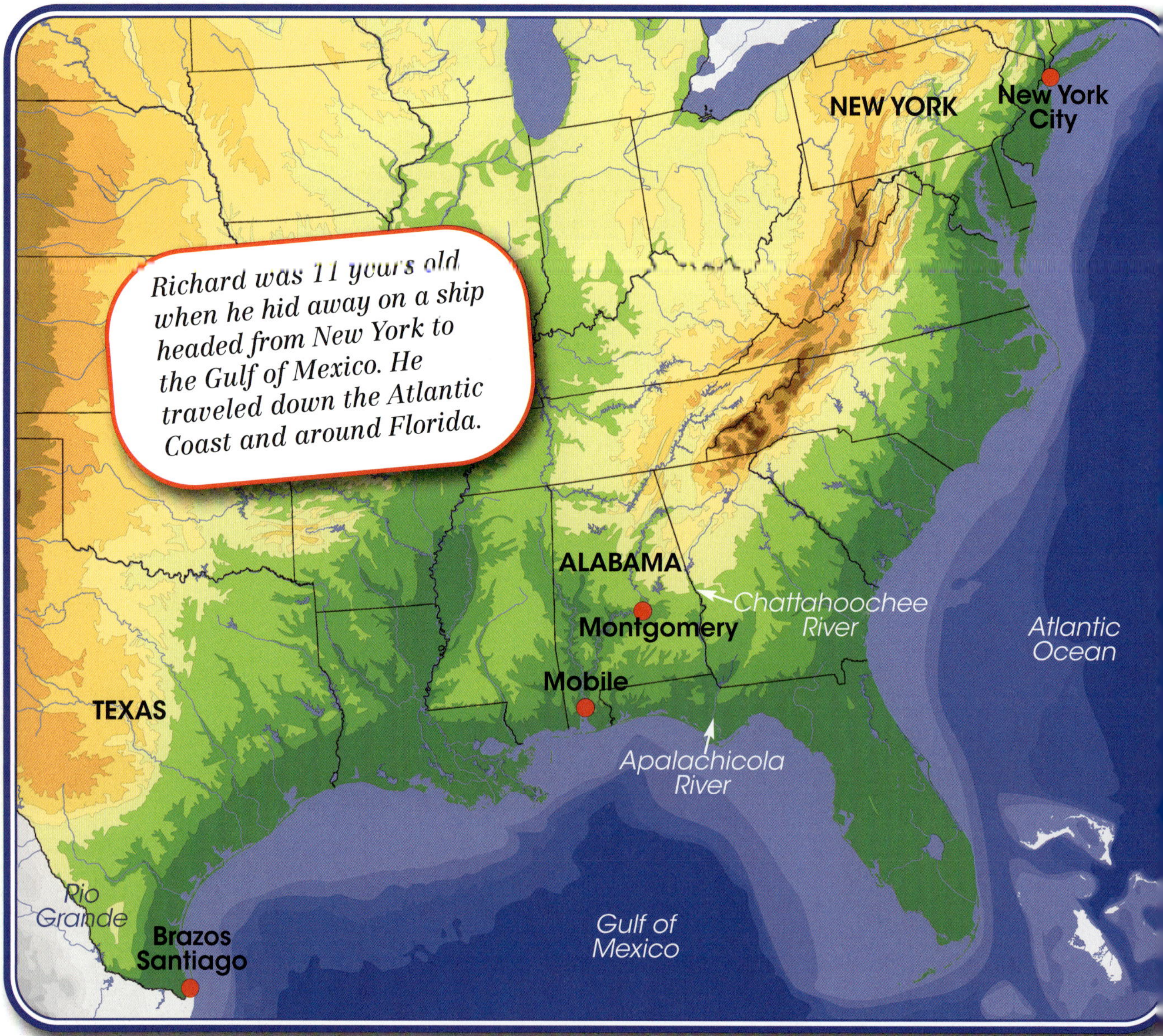

Richard was 11 years old when he hid away on a ship headed from New York to the Gulf of Mexico. He traveled down the Atlantic Coast and around Florida.

RIVERBOATING

On the trip south, Richard was discovered by the ship's crew and taken to the captain. Captain Hugh Monroe decided to teach Richard how to navigate rivers in a steamboat. When he was 13, Richard went to work on another steamboat that traveled up the Alabama River between Mobile and Montgomery. He spent six years working on Alabama rivers learning the riverboating trade. In 1842, he **enlisted** for service in the Seminole War. After the war he continued working on riverboats on the Apalachicola and Chattahoochee rivers until 1847.

Richard King became a riverboat pilot when he was 16 years old.

SEMINOLE WAR

The Seminole War has been called the fiercest war fought by the United States government against American Indians. In 1832, a group of Seminole Indians signed a **treaty** with the United States, agreeing to give up their land in Florida and move west within three years. The US Army arrived in 1835 to make sure the Seminoles left, but war broke out instead. A small band of about 3,000 Seminole warriors fought a **guerrilla** war against four US generals and 30,000 troops. The war lasted from 1835 to 1842, by which time most of the Seminoles had been moved to Indian Territory, in what is today Oklahoma.

Colonel William J. Worth took command of the US Army in Florida in May 1841. His goal was to remove all Seminoles from Florida and move them west. He would later move to Texas. The city of Fort Worth, Texas, is named after him.

▲ *Zachary Taylor spent 40 years in the US Army and fought in the Mexican War. He became president of the United States in 1849.*

MIFFLIN KENEDY

While Richard was working on riverboats in Florida, he met Mifflin Kenedy. Kenedy had been working on ships since 1834, when he had sailed to India as a cabin boy. After working briefly as a teacher and bricklayer, Kenedy began a career in river navigation. He worked on steamers on the Ohio, Missouri, and Mississippi rivers from 1836 to 1842. He worked Florida rivers from 1842 to 1846, where he met Richard. The two men became friends. During a trip to Pittsburgh, Pennsylvania, Kenedy met a US Army engineer who needed boats to transport troops fighting the Mexican War on the Texas border. Kenedy wrote to his friend Richard and invited him to Texas. In 1847, Richard decided to go.

MEXICAN WAR

The Mexican War was an armed conflict between Mexico and the United States that lasted from 1846 to 1848. Soldiers fought bloody battles at Palo Alto, Buena Vista, Churubusco, and other places in Mexico. Thousands of men died before the United States captured Mexico City and won the war. On February 2, 1848, the countries signed a peace treaty that gave California, New Mexico, Arizona, and other land to the United States. Mexico also gave up its claim to Texas and the land east of the Rio Grande.

The US Army built a base at the mouth of the Rio Grande. When war broke out between Mexico and the United States, Zachary Taylor and his troops drove the Mexican forces back.

3 TEXAS FRONTIER

When Richard King arrived in Brazos Santiago, Texas, he was 22 years old and had no money. He quickly took advantage of the opportunities, though, in the war-torn area along the border of Texas and Mexico. In June 1847, he became a second pilot on the *Colonel Cross*, then first pilot on the *Corvette*. Finally he was made captain of the *Colonel Cross*. Together, Richard and Kenedy used their riverboating experience during the remainder of the Mexican War. They transported troops and supplies to points on the Rio Grande.

M. KENEDY AND COMPANY

After the war ended, Richard, Kenedy, and another local businessman named Charles Stillman formed a steamship partnership called M. Kenedy and Company. They transported **freight** and passengers up and down the Rio Grande. Sometimes the company **smuggled** goods into Mexico. It was difficult work, but the company prospered. After a few years they were the **dominant** shipping company on the Rio Grande. Richard decided to use his profits to purchase land.

Richard designed two kinds of steamboats for use in Texas. One was used for deeper coastal waters and the other for navigating the winding, shallow Rio Grande.

Wild horses, known as mustangs, roamed free in Texas, along with buffalo and Texas longhorn cattle. Mustangs are descended from horses brought to North America by Spanish explorers in the 1500s.

WILD HORSE DESERT

In early 1852, Richard set out on a journey up the Rio Grande toward Corpus Christi. On the trip he traveled through vast grasslands where horses, buffalo, and cattle roamed free. This area was known as the Wild Horse Desert. When Richard arrived in Corpus Christi he met his friend Gideon "Legs" Lewis, a former Texas Ranger. Legs suggested they start a cow camp together. Richard would put up the money and Legs would work it and protect it. Richard knew just the place. It was 45 miles (72 km) west of Corpus Christi on the banks of the Santa Gertrudis Creek in the Wild Horse Desert.

Texas Perspective

Richard King paid less than two cents an acre (.4 ha) for his first land purchase. Some people thought he overpaid!

SANTA GERTRUDIS CREEK

In July 1853, Richard and Legs bought a piece of land along the Santa Gertrudis Creek. Originally the land had been part of a grant by the Spanish government to a Mexican named Juan Mendiola in 1834. Fear of Indian attacks and the war between Texas and Mexico in 1836 had prevented Mendiola and his family from settling on the land. Richard bought 15,500 acres (6,273 ha) of land from Mendiola's **widow** for $300.

Álvar Núñez Cabeza de Vaca, the first European to travel through Texas, wrote about the Wild Horse Desert in the 1500s:

"All over the land are vast and handsome pastures, with good grass for cattle; and it strikes me the soil would be very fertile..."

COW CAMP

One of the first tasks Richard and Legs set out to do at their cow camp was to build shelters to live in. They built a series of wood, straw, and mud huts called *jacales*. They also built corrals in which to keep the livestock. Richard purchased some cows and a bull. He also purchased a male and female horse, sheep, and goats for the camp. It was important to protect the camp from thieves. Richard and Legs added defenses, including a cannon, to protect the land. Richard also hired men to defend his land and livestock.

Some people in Brownsville called Richard's cow camp "King's Folly" because it was mostly a group of stick and grass houses known as jacales.

HISTORY OF RANCHING IN TEXAS

The tradition of herding cows on horseback began in Europe. The Spanish word for "cowhands" is *vaqueros*. The Spanish arrived in Mexico in 1521 and claimed the land for Spain. They called the area New Spain. The Spaniards brought horses and cattle to the area. The cattle the Spaniards first brought to New Spain were called criollo cattle. These cattle were bred with cattle from other parts of Europe and Great Britain. This new breed of cattle is known as Texas longhorn cattle. The Spanish also introduced their cattle-raising methods to the native Mexican people. The Spanish settled in areas of Texas in the 1600s, bringing their ranching traditions with them. The *hacienda* was an economic system based around ranching. The hacienda supplied all the needs of the workers, who lived and worked there with their families. These traditions continued after Texas won its independence from Mexico.

▲ *Mexican vaqueros worked ranches and haciendas in Mexico. Their skills and expertise on horseback made them valuable on Texas ranches.*

An average Texas longhorn can weigh 1,500 pounds (680 kg), and their horn span, from tip to tip, can be as long as 5 feet (1.5 m)!

Richard King's hacienda system was not the only one in Texas, but it became the most successful.

4 EARLY STRUGGLES

By the early 1850s, Richard had proven himself to be a successful businessman. As he began King Ranch on his Santa Gertrudis land, he realized he did not know very much about ranching. He was going to need help handling livestock. Richard respected the long-standing Mexican ranching traditions and looked south to solve his problem. In the process, he created an original ranching empire that would change Texas.

LOS KINEÑOS

In early 1854, Richard journeyed to Mexico to buy cattle. While he was there he convinced many of the people of the tiny village of Cruillas to return to Texas with him and work on the ranch. The men and women of the village brought their children, animals, and belongings with them to Texas. They became known as "Los Kineños," or "King's people."

Most ranches in Texas at the time had a foreman, slaves, and several cowhands who worked only part of the year. Richard's ranch was different. Richard provided steady work, homes, and food for Los Kineños and their families. Los Kineños, in exchange, brought expert knowledge of horses and cattle, a strong work habit, and loyalty to Richard as head of the ranch.

Texas Perspective

The Kineños tradition set King Ranch apart from other ranches in Texas. It was based on the Mexican hacienda system.

HENRIETTA KING

Henrietta Chamberlain King was born in 1832 in Boonville, Missouri. She moved to Brownsville, Texas, in 1849 where her father established the first **Presbyterian** church on the Rio Grande. Henrietta and Richard met in 1850 and he **courted** her for several years before they finally married. Henrietta's strict upbringing and strong faith proved very valuable on King Ranch. Despite hostile surroundings, Henrietta always made the ranch a welcoming place for visitors and Los Kineños. Henrietta often took care of the ranch when Richard was away, and after his death in 1885, she played a key role in the survival of King Ranch.

Richard and Henrietta married in December 1854 and had five children together.

R. KING AND COMPANY

In 1855, Legs Lewis was killed, and Richard was left to run the ranch on his own. Even though Richard had enlarged his land holdings with another 53,000 acres (21,448 ha) of grassland in 1854, he found it was difficult to make a profit. He tried many different ways. He raised Texas longhorn cattle that he sold to other ranchers. He raised horses and mules for the US Army. He even raised sheep to sell the wool. In 1860, Richard and Mifflin Kenedy partnered together again, this time in the Santa Gertrudis ranching business. They called their business R. King and Company.

WAR PROFITS

As Richard was beginning to devote more time to his ranching business, the Civil War broke out. The war was fought between Northern states, called the Union, and Southern states, called the Confederacy. Richard supported the Confederacy. He saw the war as an opportunity to make money, just as he did during the Mexican War in the 1840s. He partnered with Brownsville businessman Charles Stillman in a number of wartime ventures, including shipping salt, wool, and cotton.

COTTON

Cotton proved to be the most profitable wartime commodity for Richard. Cotton was a crop grown in Texas and other parts of the Southern United States. It was very important to the economy. The Union wanted to prevent the sale of southern cotton to other countries in order to weaken the Confederate economy so it could not afford to continue to wage war. Richard, Stillman, and Mifflin Kenedy formed a new company called Kenedy, Stillman, & King to keep the cotton flowing during the war.

Cotton was Texas's largest export. Factories in the northern United States, England, and France depended on a steady supply of cotton arriving by ship from Texas.

BLOCKADE

In April 1861, the Union announced a blockade of all Southern ports. It was designed to make life hard for the Confederacy and end their ability to fund a war.

The way the Union decided to stop cotton sales was to have navy ships block all the ports in the Southern United States. This would prevent ships from getting in or going out. However, Richard's new company had a creative way to solve this problem. Since Mexico was a neutral country during the Civil War, Mexican ships could travel along the Rio Grande without fear of being stopped by the Union navy. Richard used ships flying Mexican flags to transport the cotton to ships waiting offshore to take the cargo to markets around the world. It was called running the blockade, and Richard and his partners made a lot of money doing it.

CIVIL WAR IN TEXAS

Before the Civil War began, many Americans were arguing over the issue of slavery. Northern states passed laws that banned slavery. Southern states, including Texas, did not want to ban slavery. Southern states began holding meetings, called conventions, to discuss seceding, or leaving, the United States. They wanted to form a new country, called the Confederate States of America, that allowed slavery. In 1861, Texas voted to join the Confederacy. The Civil War was fought from 1861 to 1865. After terrible losses on both sides, the North won the war and the country was reunited. It took many years for the country to fully recover, though.

The King Ranch served as the collection point for cotton coming from other parts of Texas, and as far away as Arkansas, Louisiana, and Missouri.

UNION RAID

The Union army knew that cotton was being stored at King Ranch until it could be shipped south. On December 23, 1863, the army raided Richard's ranch. The ranch was looted, horses and possessions were stolen, and one ranch hand was killed. The army came back the following day and burned all the bales of cotton Richard had in storage at the ranch. Richard was not at home, but Henrietta's father, Hiram Chamberlain, gave an eyewitness account.

From the *Houston Tri-Weekly Telegraph*, February 1, 1864:

> ***"The people in the house offered no resistance, but the house was plundered anyway, the ladies' trunks and clothes spilled out, all the horses and mules stolen, and all the [slaves] set free..."***

PARDON

King Ranch was abandoned after the raid, and Henrietta and the children moved to San Antonio. Things were dangerous for Richard so he spent the rest of the war out of sight, although he continued to ship supplies for the Confederacy. When the Union won the war, Richard planned to move all businesses to Mexico. However, he received a **pardon** from President Andrew Johnson in late 1865 and returned to Texas to rebuild his ranch.

5 KING RANCH

Rebuilding his ranch after the Civil War was not going to be an easy thing for Richard to do. The Texas Rangers were disbanded in 1865, so there was little protection for ranchers from thieves and bandits roaming between the Rio Grande and Nueces River. Many of these bandits came from Mexico and raided Texas ranches. They stole cattle and drove them back into Mexico where they could not be recovered. Many ranchers went out of business.

It took the Texas Rangers eight months to restore order to the area.

CATTLE WARS

Thousands of cattle were lost during this time. Between 1866 and 1869, Richard reported losses of nearly 150,000 cattle from his ranches. He valued the losses at nearly $3 million! Richard was even **ambushed** on his way to give a report to the US government about how serious the raiding problem had become. When the Texas Rangers were reassembled in 1875, forces were sent to patrol the area, stop the raiders, and restore order. Rangers killed many bandits and the raids decreased. To help the situation, Mexican president Porfirio Díaz sent troops to stop the raids.

Cattle raids in Texas ended after Porfirio Díaz took control of the Mexican government in 1876. ▶

Cattle were branded so that people would know who owned them. An iron rod was heated and then applied to the skin of cattle, leaving a mark, or brand. Every ranch had its own unique brand.

A MARKET FOR BEEF

Before the Civil War the market for Texas cattle was small. Ranchers sold hides to make money, while others organized cattle drives to Louisiana or California to sell their cattle there. In 1854, cattle were sent north to Chicago and St. Louis. Since it was much cheaper to raise cattle in Texas than in other parts of the United States, things looked good for the future of Texas cattle. Once the Civil War broke out, though, all trade with the South was cut off. Many ranch owners and workers left to join the army. Texas cattle wandered the open land for four years and multiplied.

When the war ended, hundreds of thousands of cattle could be purchased in Texas for about $5 a head. The growing cities in the North were filled with new people and the demand for beef increased. Markets were willing to pay $40 a head. If Texas ranchers could get their cattle to those markets, they could make a lot of money. Richard set about collecting and **branding** the thousands of cattle that were on his land. He also ended his partnership with Mifflin Kenedy.

▶ *In 1869, Richard registered the Running W brand. It was sometimes called the "little snake" because it looked like a rattlesnake coiled on the ground.*

CATTLE DRIVES

After cattle were collected and branded, ranchers like Richard had to find ways to get the cattle 1,000 miles (1,609 km) north. In the late 1860s, cattle drives were organized and trails were **blazed**. Teams of cowhands would lead up to a thousand head of cattle at a time across the open plains. It was a long and difficult journey, but for those who made it, the reward was worth the effort. Texas longhorn cattle were well suited to make these long drives.

Legendary Texas cattleman Charles Goodnight wrote of the longhorns:

> ***"As trail cattle, their equal never has been known. Their hoofs are superior to those of any other cattle.... They can go farther without water and endure more suffering than others."***

END OF THE CATTLE DRIVES

Many of the cattle drives ended at railheads in Kansas where the cattle would be loaded onto railcars. The cattle were then shipped to Chicago and other cities in the Midwest where they would be **slaughtered**. By 1884, things had begun to change. The demand for Texas longhorns, whose beef was tougher to chew than other cattle, started to decline. More cattle were being raised in the Midwest, which meant fewer were needed from Texas. Cattle drives also got harder to make each year as more ranchers fenced off their lands. It was the establishment of railroads in Texas that finally ended the cattle drives.

Once railroads came to Texas, cattle could be loaded locally for shipment north instead of being driven up the trails to railheads in Kansas.

LIFE ON THE RANCH

As the cattle business grew, so did Richard and Henrietta's own home on the ranch. The original cow camp jacale was replaced by a one-story house. The house was built on the highest land above the Santa Gertrudis Creek, and from that spot a viewer could see the surrounding land for 20 miles (32 km). The house was expanded and enlarged during Richard's lifetime. A reporter visiting the ranch in 1874 observed that, besides the main ranch house, there were houses where about 100 Los Kineños lived, stables, and well-kept grounds. Henrietta worked hard to make life on the ranch as comfortable as possible for the family. The home was known for its hospitality and, over the years, entertained many important guests, such as judges, governors, and army officers.

In a letter to his wife, Robert E. Lee described the Kings' place in the late 1850s:

"The King cottage was removed from the street by well kept trees and shrubbery in the yard, among which were several orange trees filled with ripening fruit. Mrs. King's table was loaded with sweet oranges and many other things tempting to the eye."

General Robert E. Lee and Richard were good friends. Lee is reported to have given Richard advice to "Buy land and never sell." The Kings named their second son, Robert Lee King, in honor of the general.

CATTLE KING

The years of cattle drives made Richard even richer. He had sent thousands of cattle to Kansas during the boom years. The *Galveston News* called him "the great cattle King of Texas." Richard was not content with his past successes, though. He continued to expand his land holdings, experiment with new cattle and ways to get them to market, and improve his cattle operation.

LAND, LAND, LAND

In the 1870s, Richard bought the San Juan de Carrecitos land grant, totaling about 350,000 acres (141,640 ha). It was 60 miles (97 km) south of Santa Gertrudis. The purchases continued. In 1878, he bought 2,000 acres (809 ha). Another 18,000 acres (7,284 ha) in 1880 was followed by 25,000 acres (10,117 ha) in 1881. Richard made over sixty major land purchases in his life, totaling about 614,000 acres (248,477 ha).

Richard King once told his partner Mifflin Kenedy:

"Land and livestock have a way of increasing in value. Cattle and horse, sheep and goats, will reproduce themselves into value."

NEW BREEDS

Richard knew that Texas longhorn beef was losing favor with the northern markets. People wanted better tasting beef, so Richard began buying Durham bulls and cows from Kentucky in 1873. He started a breeding program to improve the beef he produced.

Richard helped fund a railway from Corpus Christi to Laredo. The line started running in 1881 and came within 20 miles (32 km) of Santa Gertrudis.

FENCES

Until the 1870s, most cattle roamed free. Every spring, the cattle were rounded up and sorted by brand. In the late 1860s and early 1870s, Richard was one of the first ranchers to start fencing his land in. He built his fences out of wood, which was very expensive to do. The fences helped prevent theft and improved breeding. By 1874, Richard had fenced off 70,000 acres (28,328 ha) of his land. It would take a rider 10 days on horseback to see it all. Today, there is 2,000 miles (3,219 km) of fencing at King Ranch. It could stretch all the way from Kingsville, Texas, to Boston, Massachusetts!

Texas Perspective

In 1870, Richard King was the richest man in Texas. He had 33,000 cattle on 146,000 acres (59,084 ha) of ranch land.

Barbed wire was invented in 1874. Many ranchers began using barbed wire to fence off their ranches because it was less expensive than wood.

TRAGEDY

In 1883, Richard's 19-year-old son, Robert Lee, died of pneumonia. He had been Richard's **heir** and choice to take over the business. Richard was saddened by the loss of his son and the changing nature of the Texas **frontier**. For a time he considered selling his empire. Several other ranching companies sent representatives to see Richard's cattle and the land he was considering selling. Richard decided to keep his empire, though. He had another **successor** in mind.

ROBERT JUSTUS KLEBERG II

Richard King met Robert Justus Kleberg II in 1881. At the time, Kleberg was a young lawyer in Corpus Christi who had been arguing a case against Richard. When Kleberg won the case, Richard was so impressed he offered him a job handling the ranch's legal work. Kleberg agreed, and he became one of Richard's most trusted advisors. Together they worked on many business deals. In 1885, Richard would choose him to take over the ranch.

Richard's final instruction to his lawyer before he left his ranch for the last time:

> ***"Don't let a foot of the dear old Santa Gertrudis get away from us."***

FINAL DAYS

Richard had lived a hard life on the frontier. By 1885, his health was failing badly. In February he set out from the Santa Gertrudis ranch with Henrietta to visit his doctor in San Antonio. Richard would never see his beloved ranch again. The doctor in San Antonio told him he had stomach cancer and would not live much longer. King spent his last days visiting with friends and writing his will. He died at the Menger Hotel on April 14. He was 60 years old.

On April 15, 1885, Richard King's funeral was held in San Antonio's Menger Hotel.

7 RICHARD'S LEGACY

Richard left the ranch and all his possessions to Henrietta in his will. She gave Robert Kleberg the job of running the ranch. It was going to be tough. Kleberg was a lawyer, not a rancher. He did not speak Spanish and he was only an average horse rider. On top of that, the King Ranch had many debts. With cattle prices dropping and drought gripping southern Texas, Kleberg was going to need the same kind of entrepreneurial spirit as Richard King to keep King Ranch going.

VIEW FOR THE FUTURE

Kleberg saw opportunities for more than just ranching on King's land in southern Texas. He believed there could be towns and cities, and the key to building them was getting a railroad line to connect Corpus Christi to Brownsville. Kleberg spent time and money drilling for water on the land in order to encourage railroads to build. In 1899, he found water and things began to come together. King Ranch donated land for the railway and set aside land for the town of Kingsville, which was founded in 1904. Henrietta donated land for churches and schools to be built in Kingsville. Kleberg also continued to buy land and use it to grow new crops, such as oranges and grapefruit. He also made King Ranch a leader in its cattle and horse operations.

Robert Kleberg built the first cattle-dipping vat to stop the spread of Texas tick fever. As the cattle passed through the vat, any ticks would be killed. This invention was put into use across Texas.

BIRTH OF A BREED

Since the 1870s, Richard King had been buying other types of cattle to improve the quality of the meat he sold at market. Kleberg continued and expanded Richard's breeding program. In 1910, Kleberg began crossing Brahman cattle from India with British Shorthorn cattle. After about ten years of experimenting, a red male calf was born. They called the calf Monkey because he was very playful. Monkey was the start of an entirely new breed of cattle, called the Santa Gertrudis. Monkey died in 1932, but the breeding continued. In 1940 Santa Gertrudis cattle were officially recognized as a breed.

Texas Perspective

King Ranch developed the first breed of American cattle, called the Santa Gertrudis.

The Santa Gertrudis breed suits the harsh conditions of southern Texas while still providing fine quality beef. It is now popular around the world.

ECONOMIC IMPACT

At its height, King Ranch held more than 1.15 million acres (607,028 ha) of land in Texas. Today it covers 825,000 acres (333,866 ha), which is an area larger than the state of Rhode Island, and maintains other ranches around the world. Besides breeding cattle and horses, King Ranch is also a leader in teaching ranch management. The ranch also contributes to the Texas economy by licensing oil and gas rights on its land.

When Richard King died, a newspaper wrote, "His history is almost a history of this frontier." The King Ranch continues to live up to that tradition today. The ranch has a museum where people can learn about the history of Texas ranching.

LEARNING MORE

BOOKS

James, Trisha. *Cattle and Oil: The Growth of Texas Industries*. New York: The Rosen Publishing Group, 2010.

Sanford, William R., and Carl R. Green. *Richard King: Courageous Texas Cattleman*. Courageous Heroes of the American West. Berkeley Heights, NJ: Enslow Publishers, 2013.

WEBSITES @

Cattle Raisers Museum
www.cattleraisersmuseum.org

Kenedy Ranch Museum
www.kenedymuseum.org

King Ranch
www.king-ranch.com

TIMELINE

Texas | Richard King

- **1824** Richard King is born in New York on July 10
- **1833** Goes to work for a jeweler in Manhattan
- **1835** Runs away; takes a ship south to the Gulf of Mexico and works on riverboats in Alabama
- **1840** Becomes a steamboat pilot
- **1842** Meets Mifflin Kenedy during the Seminole Wars in Florida
- **1846** The United States and Mexico fight the Mexican War until 1848; Texas becomes 28th state in the United States
- **1847** Moves to Texas to pilot troops up the Rio Grande during the Mexican War
- **1850** Partners in a steamboat company, M. Kenedy and Co; meets Henrietta Chamberlain
- **1852** Travels north from the Rio Grande to Corpus Christi and travels to the Wild Horse Desert
- **1853** Purchases land where the town of Kingsville now stands
- **1854** Purchases more land in the Wild Horse Desert; convinces a Mexican village to follow him to Texas to work on his ranch as Kineños; marries Henrietta in December
- **1860** Partners with Kenedy in the Santa Gertrudis ranch
- **1861** On March 1, 1861, Texas joins the Confederate States of America. Civil War begins on April 12, 1861. Richard supports the Confederates against the Union
- **1863** Ranch is raided by Union troops
- **1865** Rebuilds ranch after Union defeats the Confederacy
- **1869** Registers the Running W brand
- **1870** Dissolves partnership with Kenedy; begins a cattle breeding program and continues to buy more land; drives cattle north to Kansas until 1884
- **1881** Meets Robert Kleberg
- **1885** Richard King dies at the Menger Hotel in San Antonio, on April 14
- **1904** Town of Kingsville established and named for Richard

GLOSSARY

ambushed (AM-bushd) Attacked by surprise from a hiding place.
apprentice (uh-PREN-tis) A person who learns a trade by working for someone who is already trained.
blazed (BLAYZD) Marked out or cleared a new trail.
branding (BRAND-ing) Burning with a hot iron to mark something to show ownership.
courted (KORT-ed) Tried to gain another's interest.
dominant (DAH-mih-nent) Most important and successful.
empire (EM-pyr) A large area controlled by one leader.
enlisted (in-LIST-ed) Joined the armed forces.
freight (FRAYT) Goods carried by wagon or boat to either a merchant or a customer.
frontier (frun-TEER) The edge of a settled country, where the wilderness begins.
guerrilla (guh-RIL-uh) Describing a small, defensive force of irregular soldiers.
heir (AYR) Someone who gets a person's property after the person has died.
hostile (HAHS-tul) Unfriendly, like an enemy.
pardon (PAR-dun) To excuse someone who did something wrong.
Presbyterian (prez-bih-TEER-ee-un) Of or relating to a branch of the Christian church.
slaughtered (SLAH-terd) Killed in large numbers.
smuggled (SMUH-guld) Sneaked something banned into or out of the country.
successor (suk-SEH-ser) Someone who takes over the leadership role when the current leader steps down or dies.
treaty (TREE-tee) An official agreement, signed and agreed upon by each party.
widow (WIH-doh) A woman whose husband has died.

INDEX